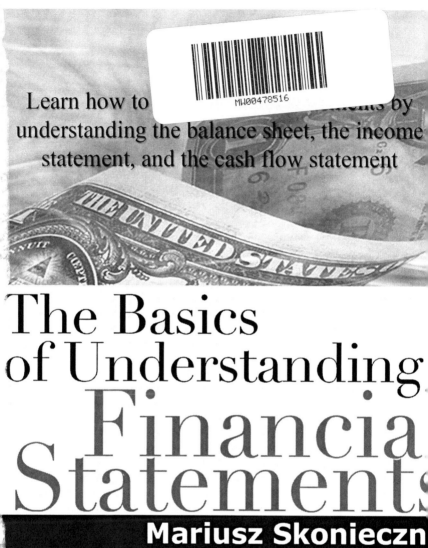

Learn how to [   ] by understanding the balance sheet, the income statement, and the cash flow statement

The Basics
of Understanding
Financia
Statements

Mariusz Skonieczn

Classic Value Investors, LL

The Basics of Understanding Financial Statements

Learn how to read financial statements by understanding the balance sheet, the income statement, and the cash flow statement

Written by
Mariusz Skonieczny

Investment Publishing
Schaumburg, IL

Printed by Investment Publishing
Schaumburg, IL

First printing 2012
Printed in the United States of America

15 14 13 12

ISBN 978-0-9848490-0-0

Cover design and interior page layout by:
Lucie Allam of graphi-co.com

Table
of Contents

Acknowledgments

I am grateful to all the individuals who helped me with the book. First, I would like to thank my editors C. Daniel Miller and Joyce L. Miller of Integrated Writer Services. Second, I would like to thank Lucie Allam of Graphi-Co.com for the design of the book cover and interior pages. Finally, I would like to thank Mary Jester and Roger Dabdab for reading the original manuscript and providing me with their valuable feedback.

Preface:
Financial
Statements

Financial Statements

❝❝Jeśli rozwiniesz swoje umiejętności inwestycyjne i jeśli inwestujesz mądrze, to pozwoli Ci to w przyszłości żyć lepiej i zapewnisz sobie w ten sposób godną emeryturę na przyszłość. Niestety większość ludzi nie ma ochoty uczyć się jak inwestować swoje pieniądze, więc dlatego ufają na ślepo tak zwanym profesjonalistom, którzy są ubrani w drogie i eleganckie garnitury, są dobrze uczesani i pięknie mówią. Drogę, którą wybierzesz, zależy wyłącznie od Ciebie.❞❞

It is unlikely that anyone would disagree that in order to understand the text above, one has to know the language in which it is written. Unfortunately, many investors do not transfer this logic to the field of investing. Many people choose to invest their entire life savings into stocks, yet they do not take the time to learn basic accounting, which is the language of business.

Managers of publicly traded companies communicate with shareholders about the successes and failures of their business endeavors through financial statements which include the balance sheet, the income statement, and the cash flow statement. The preparation of financial statements is guided by various accounting guidelines. When buyers and sellers of stocks are truly involved in buying and selling businesses, it is critical that they know how to read and understand financial statements so that they know what it is that they are buying or selling. The purpose of my other book, *Why Are We So Clueless about the Stock Market,* is to help investors build a basic investment foundation. It is targeted toward beginning and intermediate investors who might not have had much investment experience. This book, on the other hand, requires readers to know information covered in *Why Are We So Clueless about the*

Stock Market. This book is intended to take investors to the next level by equipping them with the knowledge necessary to read financial statements.

This book is not intended to cover all the possible topics in accounting and financial statement preparation. Coverage of such a complex subject would require a work much broader in scope and much more voluminous than this primer. However, investors do not need to become professional accountants in order to have the skills necessary to make competent investment decisions – what is necessary is a basic understanding of accounting. The ability to understand basic accounting in order to read financial statements is just another tool in the toolbox for wise investors. It does not guarantee investment success; however, its lack almost certainly guarantees failure.

Balance
Sheet

Chapter 1

Balance Sheet

The balance sheet is a financial statement that shows what a company owns, how much it owes, and what is left for the shareholders in the form of equity. This same approach can be taken by homeowners who own an asset called a home. In this case, they might owe 90 percent of the value to the bank, while the remaining 10 percent represents equity. The balance sheet shows the company's financial position on a particular day, such as March 31 for the end of first quarter or December 31 for the end of the year. The balance sheet can be thought of as a photograph of the company's financial situation at a particular point of time. Its preparation is based on the most important accounting equation:

$$\text{ASSETS} = \text{LIABILITIES} + \text{EQUITY}$$

The reason this financial statement is called a balance sheet is due to the fact that the accounting equation has to balance all the time. It means that assets must always be  equal to liabilities plus equity. This makes sense even at an individual's level because all possessions (assets) are either owned free and clear (equity) or purchased by acquiring debt (liabilities). A home buyer's down payment is an example of equity, while the mortgage is an example of debt.

Figure 1 shows an example of a balance sheet and the concept of how assets ($95,309) equal liabilities ($31,629) plus equity ($63,680).

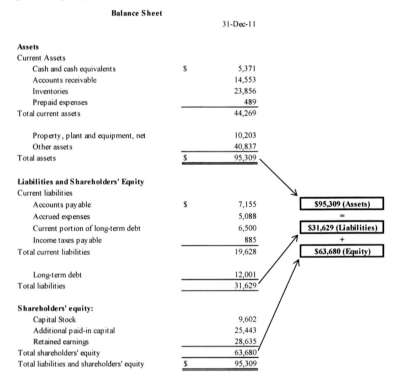

Balance Sheet

		31-Dec-11
Assets		
Current Assets		
Cash and cash equivalents	$	5,371
Accounts receivable		14,553
Inventories		23,856
Prepaid expenses		489
Total current assets		44,269
Property, plant and equipment, net		10,203
Other assets		40,837
Total assets	$	95,309
Liabilities and Shareholders' Equity		
Current liabilities		
Accounts payable	$	7,155
Accrued expenses		5,088
Current portion of long-term debt		6,500
Income taxes payable		885
Total current liabilities		19,628
Long-term debt		12,001
Total liabilities		31,629
Shareholders' equity:		
Capital Stock		9,602
Additional paid-in capital		25,443
Retained earnings		28,635
Total shareholders' equity		63,680
Total liabilities and shareholders' equity	$	95,309

$95,309 (Assets)
=
$31,629 (Liabilities)
+
$63,680 (Equity)

Figure 1

The date in the upper right corner of Figure 1 indicates that this balance sheet is for December 31.

ASSETS

Assets represent tangible items that the company owns such as cash, inventory, machinery, and intangible items such patents, copyrights, franchises, trademarks, and goodwill. Assets are classified into current assets; property, plant and equipment (PP&E); and other assets.

CURRENT ASSETS

Current assets, which consist of cash and cash equivalents, accounts receivable, inventory, and prepaid expenses, are called "current" because they are expected to be either converted into cash or their benefit received (in the case of prepaid expenses) within 12 months. These items are listed according to their liquidity, meaning that the most liquid assets, such as cash, are listed first.

Balance Sheet

		31-Dec-11
Assets		
Current Assets		
Cash and cash equivalents	$	5,371
Accounts receivable		14,553
Inventories		23,856
Prepaid expenses		489
Total current assets		44,269
Property, plant and equipment, net		10,203
Other assets		40,837
Total assets	$	95,309

Figure 2

Current assets are part of the current asset cycle, and are also called "working assets" because a certain amount of cash is constantly being spent on inventory and is turned back into cash after customers pay for a company's products or services.

CASH AND CASH EQUIVALENTS

Cash represents coins, paper bills, and on-demand bank deposits. Cash equivalents represent highly liquid, very safe, and short-term investments such as certificates of deposits, Treasury bills, and money market funds.

Balance Sheet

		31-Dec-11
Assets		
Current Assets		
Cash and cash equivalents	$	5,371
Accounts receivable		14,553
Inventories		23,856
Prepaid expenses		489
Total current assets		44,269
Property, plant and equipment, net		10,203
Other assets		40,837
Total assets	$	95,309

Figure 3

A good way to analyze cash and cash equivalents is to compare them to total assets from quarter to quarter and year to year. For example, if every year for the past 10 years, cash and cash equivalents constituted 5 to 7 percent of total assets and this percentage jumps to 20 percent, this incident should be investigated more closely. Such a jump may be positive or negative, depending on where the cash came from. If the cash came from the company's operations, indicated by a sudden increase in retained earnings, which will be discussed later, this could mean that the company became more profitable. If the cash increase was a result of the company selling one of its properties, taking on more debt, or issuing more shares, it may not be good for shareholders because fewer properties may translate into a reduced ability to generate revenue in the future, more debt will increase interest payments, and more outstanding shares will dilute the interests of current shareholders.

Even when cash comes from operations, the wisest course of action may not be to stockpile cash. It is the management's job to put it to work or return it to the shareholders in the form of dividends or share buybacks.

ACCOUNTS RECEIVABLE

The accounts receivable account on the balance sheet represents the amount of money that the company's customers owe to the company. This account is necessary because many businesses do not receive cash upon the shipment of goods or delivery of services, but instead extend credit to its customers with terms typically of 30 to 60 days. Under accounting guidelines, when the product is shipped to the customer, a sale is recorded and accounts receivable is increased. Cash changes hands only when the customer actually pays.

Balance Sheet

		31-Dec-11
Assets		
Current Assets		
Cash and cash equivalents	$	5,371
Accounts receivable		14,553
Inventories		23,856
Prepaid expenses		489
Total current assets		44,269
Property, plant and equipment, net		10,203
Other assets		40,837
Total assets	$	95,309

Figure 4

It is important to monitor accounts receivable because a company may be reporting increasing sales, yet if it fails to collect accounts receivable, it could be in trouble. The state of the relationship between accounts receivable to total net sales could serve as a warning sign that something is wrong. A sudden jump in accounts receivable in relation to net sales may mean that the company is having a tough time collecting from its customers, is extending credit to weaker customers, or is extending credit to current customers in order to make its sales targets.

INVENTORY

Inventory is what the company produces or buys to sell to its customers. While cash is the same for all businesses operating with the same currency, inventory composition is different depending on the type of business.

Balance Sheet

		31-Dec-11
Assets		
Current Assets		
Cash and cash equivalents	$	5,371
Accounts receivable		14,553
Inventories		23,856
Prepaid expenses		489
Total current assets		44,269
Property, plant and equipment, net		10,203
Other assets		40,837
Total assets	$	95,309

Figure 5

For example, Arctic Cat, a manufacturer of snowmobiles and all-terrain vehicles (ATVs), has different items in its inventory account than a restaurant does.

However, inventory may consist of more than just finished products and is divided into three categories: raw materials, work-in-progress, and finished goods. Raw materials are the most basic materials used in the production of products. Work-in-progress represents products that are not yet finished, but are past the raw materials stage.

Depending on the business, a company's inventory could become obsolete. This is where management skills come into play. If a restaurant manager orders more tomatoes than needed, they will rot and shareholders' capital will be wasted. The same principle applies to manufacturers. Arctic Cat should not produce more snowmobiles than the market demands because they are not going to sell or will have to be discounted significantly to be converted to cash through the current asset cycle.

PREPAID EXPENSES

Prepaid expenses are expenditures that have already been made for benefits that the company will receive in the near future. Examples of prepaid expenses are advances for insurance policies, rent, and taxes. Prepaid expenses are classified as current assets, not because they can be turned into cash, but because if they had not been prepaid, that cash would have to be spent within 12 months. Some prepaid expenses also result in cost savings, such as paying insurance premiums annually instead of monthly.

Balance Sheet

		31-Dec-11
Assets		
Current Assets		
Cash and cash equivalents	$	5,371
Accounts receivable		14,553
Inventories		23,856
Prepaid expenses		489
Total current assets		44,269
Property, plant and equipment, net		10,203
Other assets		40,837
Total assets	$	95,309

Figure 6

PROPERTY, PLANT AND EQUIPMENT

Property, plant and equipment (PP&E) is a term that refers to all of the company's assets that are not intended to be sold or resold to customers. Items in this account are also referred to as "fixed assets." These assets are used on a repeated basis to provide services or manufacture products.

Balance Sheet

		31-Dec-11
Assets		
Current Assets		
Cash and cash equivalents	$	5,371
Accounts receivable		14,553
Inventories		23,856
Prepaid expenses		489
Total current assets		44,269
Property, plant and equipment, net		10,203
Other assets		40,837
Total assets	$	95,309

Figure 7

The most common fixed assets include land, buildings, machinery, furniture, and tools. The composition of fixed assets depends on the type of business. For example, International Speedway Corporation, a leading promoter of NASCAR racing events, would have speedway facilities in the property, plant and equipment asset category.

Exxon Mobil Corporation, on the other hand, would show different types of assets in its property, plant and equipment account such as oil and gas reserves, pipelines, and tankers.

When fixed assets are purchased, they are reported at cost on the balance sheet. Because they are expected to be used over many years, their expenditures are not charged against income during the year of purchase. Only a pro rata part of their cost based on their estimated useful life is charged every year as a depreciation expense. The reduction in the value of the asset is recorded in an account called accumulated depreciation. The net amount for property, plant and equipment is achieved after subtracting accumulated depreciation from the fixed assets' original cost as shown below.

Property, plant and equipment at cost	$10,000,000
Accumulated depreciation	$4,000,000
Property, plant and equipment at cost, net	$6,000,000

In general, because fixed assets are repeatedly used by companies to generate revenues, the more of these assets that a company owns, the more money it can generate. However, the fact that these assets are categorized by accounting standards as assets on the balance sheet does not necessarily mean that they are true assets from the investors' and owners' points of view. For example, a 100-unit apartment building can be a great asset generating steady cash flow for its owners during times of high occupancy. However, the same apartment building is a drag on owners' finances when vacant or at low occupancy because certain fixed expenses, such as taxes and insurance, have to be paid regardless of the level of occupancy. The same concept applies to a business – if a business owns an asset that consumes cash instead of creating it, this asset is more of a liability than an asset, no matter how it is categorized by accountants.

Companies that have to keep upgrading and replacing property, plant and equipment assets just to stay competitive are in worse shape than those that can keep using these assets until they completely wear out. Money that has to be spent on replacing assets cannot be used on more advantageous purposes that actually benefit shareholders such as buying more equipment, acquiring other companies, paying down debt, paying dividends, and repurchasing shares.

International Speedway Corporation is a perfect example of this concept because speedway facilities do not have to constantly be replaced. They have to be maintained and upgraded, but in comparison to the company's revenues, it is not a great burden. Over the last two decades as NASCAR became the second most-watched sport on TV after football, International Speedway Corporation made significant capital expenditures that expanded the seating capacity of its speedways. The additional seating capacity increased the company's earning potential because of the potential to sell more tickets.

In order to analyze how much money is spent on replacing and upgrading existing fixed assets, it is necessary to analyze the property, plant and equipment account on the balance sheet over many years, to read annual reports, and to analyze the cash flow statement, which is discussed in a separate chapter.

OTHER ASSETS

Other assets are assets that do not really fit into current assets or property, plant and equipment. They include items such as patents, copyrights, goodwill, trademarks, trade names, secret processes, and noncurrent receivables.

Balance Sheet

		31-Dec-11
Assets		
Current Assets		
Cash and cash equivalents	$	5,371
Accounts receivable		14,553
Inventories		23,856
Prepaid expenses		489
Total current assets		44,269
Property, plant and equipment, net		10,203
Other assets		40,837
Total assets	$	95,309

Figure 8

LIABILITIES

Liabilities represent what the company owes to various groups or businesses such as employees, suppliers, customers, creditors, and governments. Liabilities are categorized into current liabilities and long-term liabilities.

CURRENT LIABILITIES

Current liabilities are the company's obligations that are due within 12 months. The most basic current liabilities are accounts payable, accrued expenses, current portion of long-term debt, and income taxes payable. This section of the balance sheet from Figure 1 is illustrated in Figure 9 below.

Balance Sheet

		31-Dec-11
Liabilities and Shareholders' Equity		
Current liabilities		
Accounts payable	$	7,155
Accrued expenses		5,088
Current portion of long-term debt		6,500
Income taxes payable		885
Total current liabilities	$	19,628

Figure 9

ACCOUNTS PAYABLE

Accounts payable represents amounts that a company owes its vendors or suppliers for which an invoice has been received.

Balance Sheet

		31-Dec-11
Liabilities and Shareholders' Equity		
Current liabilities		
Accounts payable	$	7,155
Accrued expenses		5,088
Current portion of long-term debt		6,500
Income taxes payable		885
Total current liabilities	$	19,628

Figure 10

As mentioned before, businesses offer various credit terms to each other. One company's accounts receivable under assets is another company's accounts payable under liabilities. Many investors have a negative perception of liabilities because they have been taught that owing someone money is irresponsible. As previously described, some assets might not necessarily be assets from the owners' point of view because they consume capital. The same principle applies to liabilities – they are not necessarily always negative. For example, Walmart is able to sell many of its products to the end user and collect cash before it pays off its accounts payable. Suppliers are effectively lending money to

Walmart for free, while Walmart turns around and makes a profit on this money before repaying it.

ACCRUED EXPENSES

Accrued expenses are obligations to pay for products or services that are already received but for which an invoice has not been received. Once an invoice is received, an accrued expense becomes an account payable. Expenses can be accrued for various items such as employees' salaries, sales tax, rent, attorneys' fees, and interest on debt.

Balance Sheet

		31-Dec-11
Liabilities and Shareholders' Equity		
Current liabilities		
Accounts payable	$	7,155
Accrued expenses		5,088
Current portion of long-term debt		6,500
Income taxes payable		885
Total current liabilities	$	19,628

Figure 11

CURRENT PORTION OF LONG-TERM DEBT

The current portion of long-term debt is the amount of debt that matures, or is due, within 12 months. For example, if the company has $5,000,000 in debt and 20 percent of it matures every year, $1,000,000 would be reported as the current portion of long-term debt under the current liabilities section every year. It is important to note that this only includes the reduction of principal; it does not include the interest expense. The interest portion is included in accrued expenses.

Balance Sheet

		31-Dec-11
Liabilities and Shareholders' Equity		
Current liabilities		
Accounts payable	$	7,155
Accrued expenses		5,088
Current portion of long-term debt		6,500
Income taxes payable		885
Total current liabilities	$	19,628

Figure 12

INCOME TAXES PAYABLE

Income taxes payable is an obligation to the government. When a company sells a product and records a profit, a percentage of it needs to be paid as income tax. The reason it is reported as a liability on the balance sheet is that it is not paid immediately after the sale but is retained by the company, usually until the quarter ends.

Balance Sheet

		31-Dec-11
Liabilities and Shareholders' Equity		
Current liabilities		
Accounts payable	$	7,155
Accrued expenses		5,088
Current portion of long-term debt		6,500
Income taxes payable		885
Total current liabilities	$	19,628

Figure 13

CURRENT RATIO

Because current assets are expected to be converted into cash within 12 months, they are used to satisfy obligations under current liabilities. Investors and analysts use a popular measure called the current ratio to determine whether the company has enough current assets to satisfy current liabilities. The current ratio measures short-term liquidity and is calculated by dividing current assets by current liabilities as shown in the following formula:

**CURRENT RATIO
=
CURRENT ASSETS/CURRENT LIABILITIES**

A current ratio greater than one indicates that the company has more current assets than current liabilities. While this may mean that the company has enough liquidity to cover short-term bills, a current ratio of less than one does not always indicate that the company faces liquidity problems. Some companies such as Coca-Cola or Walmart have current ratios of less than one because they can either easily access short-term credit or their earning power allows them to cover their short-term bills.

LONG-TERM LIABILITIES

Another type of liability is long-term debt, as shown in Figure 14.

Balance Sheet

		31-Dec-11
Liabilities and Shareholders' Equity		
Current liabilities		
Accounts payable	$	7,155
Accrued expenses		5,088
Current portion of long-term debt		6,500
Income taxes payable		885
Total current liabilities		19,628
Long-term debt		12,001
Total liabilities		31,629
Shareholders' equity:		
Capital Stock		9,602
Additional paid-in capital		25,443
Retained earnings		28,635
Total shareholders' equity		63,680
Total liabilities and shareholders' equity	$	95,309

Figure 14

Long-term liabilities are the company's obligations that are not expected to be due and paid within 12 months. Some examples of long-term liabilities include loans, lease obligations, and pension obligations.

In addition to these examples, long-term debt also includes bonds, mortgage bonds, and junk bonds. Some companies are so profitable that they do not need much debt because their internally generated funds are not only enough to operate and finance growth, but also to pay dividends.

However, as previously mentioned, not all debt is bad. If a company can borrow money at 4 percent and generate 20 percent profit on that borrowed capital, it benefits shareholders. However, the worst debt is incurred when a company does not generate enough money internally and has to borrow for regular operating expenditures in order to stay competitive. This type of debt would not produce any incremental income, and interest payments on this debt would cut into the company's profit.

A quick way to check to see if the company has taken on too much debt is to compare its net income to its total debt. If it would take twenty years to repay this debt (a situation many airline companies and auto manufacturers are often in), it would not be a good sign. However, if the company could pay it off in less than five years, then the debt level would probably not be a concern.

SHAREHOLDERS' EQUITY

Shareholders' equity is what is left after total liabilities are subtracted from total assets. This is similar to equity in a house, which is equal to the value of the house minus the mortgage.

Investors may refer to shareholders' equity as net worth or book value. It is important to analyze shareholders' equity because when buying stocks, investors are really buying the company's assets and assuming its liabilities. In other words, they are buying the shareholders' equity. It is useful to know how much they are paying for one dollar of shareholders' equity.

The three basic categories included in shareholders' equity are capital stock, additional paid-in capital, and retained earnings.

CAPITAL STOCK AND ADDITIONAL PAID-IN CAPITAL

Capital stock and additional paid-in capital represent the original capital invested into the business and any additional funds added later. Capital stock is, in most instances, shown as common stock, but at times it can also be shown as other types of stock, such as preferred stock.

Balance Sheet

		31-Dec-11
Liabilities and Shareholders' Equity		
Current liabilities		
Accounts payable	$	7,155
Accrued expenses		5,088
Current portion of long-term debt		6,500
Income taxes payable		885
Total current liabilities		19,628
Long-term debt		12,001
Total liabilities		31,629
Shareholders' equity:		
Capital Stock		9,602
Additional paid-in capital		25,443
Retained earnings		28,635
Total shareholders' equity		63,680
Total liabilities and shareholders' equity	$	95,309

Figure 15

When a company issues 1,000,000 shares of common stock and, as a result, raises $5,000,000, the balance sheet could show this transaction in the following manner:

Common Stock, $0.01 par value, 1,000,000 shares issued	**$10,000**
Additional paid-in capital	**$4,990,000**

The sum of common stock and additional paid-in capital is still $5,000,000, but because this particular stock offering was arbitrarily assigned a par value of $0.01, the amounts are separated between the two accounts. Additional paid-in capital represents a premium, and in some instances, it could be a discount over the par value. Par value plus the premium is what the original investors paid for one share of stock.

RETAINED EARNINGS

The retained earnings category represents profits that a company generated and did not pay out as dividends. It is the enterprise's undistributed profits from all years in operation, not just a single year.

Balance Sheet

	31-Dec-11
Liabilities and Shareholders' Equity	
Current liabilities	
Accounts payable	$ 7,155
Accrued expenses	5,088
Current portion of long-term debt	6,500
Income taxes payable	885
Total current liabilities	19,628
Long-term debt	12,001
Total liabilities	31,629
Shareholders' equity:	
Capital Stock	9,602
Additional paid-in capital	25,443
Retained earnings	28,635
Total shareholders' equity	63,680
Total liabilities and shareholders' equity	$ 95,309

Figure 16

When a company generates higher and higher retained earnings year after year, it is a good sign because it means that the enterprise is profitable and those retained earnings can be used to internally finance the purchase of more assets which, in turn, can increase profitability even more.

SUMMARY

The balance sheet shows the assets that businesses own, liabilities that they owe, and equity that is left for shareholders. Even though some items are considered assets and others are considered liabilities by accounting standards, they may be viewed differently from the points of view of the owners and investors. When purchasing private businesses, the new owners acquire both the assets and the liabilities. Buyers of stocks should view ownership of public companies in the same way, and by understanding how to read the balance sheet, they are able to recognize what it is that they are receiving and how much it is worth after liabilities are taken into account.

Income
Statement

Chapter 2

Income Statement

The income statement is an important financial report that shows an enterprise's success in terms of profitability. Unlike the balance sheet, the income statement is prepared for a given period such as a quarter or a year, versus a snapshot on a particular day. The preparation of this financial report is based on the following formula:

REVENUES - EXPENSES = PROFIT or LOSS

If the business brings in more revenues than it pays out in expenses, it reports a profit. Otherwise, it reports a loss. The following is a sample income statement.

Income Statement

		31-Dec-11
Revenues	$	109,017
Cost of goods sold		73,445
Gross profit		35,572
Operating expenses:		
Selling, general and administrative		22,635
Research and development		3,199
Depreciation		1,123
Operating income		8,615
Interest expense		805
Other (income)/expense, net		-87
Income before income taxes		7,897
Provision for income taxes		2,764
Net income	$	5,133
Basic earnings per share	$	0.82
Diluted earnings per share	$	0.81
Weighted average shares outstanding:		
Basic		6,286
Diluted		6,343

Figure 17

REVENUES

Revenues, also referred to as the "top line," are recorded when the company earns them by either shipping the product or completing a service. As mentioned before, the majority of businesses extend credit to their customers, and therefore, when revenues are recorded, the accounts receivable total on the balance sheet is increased and cash changes hands only when the customer pays the bill.

Income Statement

		31-Dec-11
Revenues	$	109,017
Cost of goods sold		73,445
Gross profit		35,572
Operating expenses:		
Selling, general and administrative		22,635
Research and development		3,199
Depreciation		1,123
Operating income		8,615
Interest expense		805
Other (income)/expense, net		-87
Income before income taxes		7,897
Provision for income taxes		2,764
Net income	$	5,133

Figure 18

When investors examine revenues, two of the most important characteristics they need to look for are the quality and the dependability of the revenues. A company could show increasing revenues by extending generous credit terms to its customers, and instead of collecting the cash payments, they could record an increase in accounts receivable. However, this type of revenue would not be dependable, and as a result, it would not be worth as much. The sources of revenues are key here, and to determine them, investors usually have to do more research beyond simply reading the income statement. While reading the full annual report is necessary, a phone call to one of the company's customers can shine a light on the dependability of a certain revenue stream.

Some businesses possess revenue streams that are more reliable than others. For example, cell phone or cable companies receive recurring monthly payments for their services. This type of income is extremely reliable. Now, compare this payment structure to a hair salon catering to women. As a discretionary expense, customers can easily delay or cancel hair appointments, switch to less expensive salons, or eliminate particular services such as hair coloring. A similar type of business is personal training. As another discretionary expense, customers can easily cancel or discontinue sessions.

COST OF GOODS SOLD

The cost of goods sold represents the direct expenditures associated with manufacturing a product. These expenditures include the raw materials, labor, and manufacturing overhead. When reselling a product, the cost of goods sold represents the cost of purchasing it from the manufacturer. When the company provides a service instead of selling a product, the cost of goods sold is replaced with another term – the cost of revenue.

Income Statement

		31-Dec-11
Revenues	$	109,017
Cost of goods sold		73,445
Gross profit		35,572
Operating expenses:		
Selling, general and administrative		22,635
Research and development		3,199
Depreciation		1,123
Operating income		8,615
Interest expense		805
Other (income)/expense, net		-87
Income before income taxes		7,897
Provision for income taxes		2,764
Net income	$	5,133

Figure 19

What is important to note is that the cost of goods sold only appears on the income statement when the company is actually "selling" or "reselling" its products or services. What if the company is not able to sell its products? The cost of goods sold does not appear on the income statement because the preparation of financial statements of publicly traded companies has to adhere to GAAP (Generally Accepted Accounting Principles). Under GAAP, companies must follow accrual basis accounting, which means that expenses must be matched with corresponding revenues. If the company is not able to sell its products, it does not have any revenues for the corresponding costs to be matched to, and therefore, the production costs are not expensed through the cost of goods sold on the income statement.

Investors can prevent unpleasant surprises by monitoring inventory levels on the balance sheet and comparing them to total assets and revenues. A significant accumulation of products in inventory without a similar increase in revenues may mean that the company is unable to sell it products, and as a result, may need to write down the inventory costs through the income statement as a loss without a corresponding increase in revenues.

GROSS PROFIT

Gross profit is calculated by subtracting the cost of goods sold from revenues. It is an useful measurement because it shows how efficiently the company manufactures its products. It is necessary to understand that gross profit only includes the costs that are directly associated with either producing or purchasing a product or providing a service. It does not include expenses associated with running the business such as advertising, the management's salaries, and administrative expenditures.

Income Statement

		31-Dec-11
Revenues	$	109,017
Cost of goods sold		73,445
Gross profit		35,572
Operating expenses:		
Selling, general and administrative		22,635
Research and development		3,199
Depreciation		1,123
Operating income		8,615
Interest expense		805
Other (income)/expense, net		-87
Income before income taxes		7,897
Provision for income taxes		2,764
Net income	$	5,133

Figure 20

Gross profit can be used to calculate the gross profit margin, which is useful for making side-by-side comparisons among a subject company's current manufacturing efficiency, its past manufacturing efficiency, and that of its competitors.

Companies in highly competitive industries and companies in weaker competitive positions tend to have low gross profit margins because they are forced to cut prices to stay competitive. If the company can consistently generate higher profit margins than its competitors, this may be an indication that it is benefiting from some type of competitive advantage. Gross profit margin is calculated by the following formula.

GROSS PROFIT MARGIN = GROSS PROFIT/ REVENUES

Using numbers from Figure 20, we arrive with the following results.

GROSS PROFIT MARGIN = 35,572/109,017 = 32.6%

There are ways that businesses can improve their gross profit margins. The most obvious one is to increase the prices of their products and services. On the cost side, they can find ways to use less direct labor, redesign its products so that fewer raw materials are needed, or lower manufacturing overhead by acquiring/leasing newer and more efficient manufacturing facilities. The pursuit to increase gross profit margins or prevent them from eroding was the main reason many U.S. companies chose to outsource their manufacturing activities to countries such as China where labor costs are lower than in the U.S.

OPERATING EXPENSES

Operating expenses refer to the expenditures associated with operating or running a business. They are necessary in order for the company to produce revenues. They are the muscle that makes things happen. Operating expenses consist of selling, general and administrative expenses (SG&A); research and development; and depreciation.

Income Statement

	31-Dec-11
Revenues	$ 109,017
Cost of goods sold	73,445
Gross profit	35,572
Operating expenses:	
Selling, general and administrative	22,635
Research and development	3,199
Depreciation	1,123
Operating income	8,615
Interest expense	805
Other (income)/expense, net	-87
Income before income taxes	7,897
Provision for income taxes	2,764
Net income	$ 5,133

Figure 21

SELLING, GENERAL AND ADMINISTRATIVE EXPENSES (SG&A)

Selling, general and administrative expenses (SG&A) include expenditures such as sales commissions, management salaries, office supplies, advertising, and accounting and legal fees. The amount of SG&A expenses does not mean much by itself, but becomes more meaningful when compared either to total revenues or gross profits.

Income Statement

		31-Dec-11
Revenues	$	109,017
Cost of goods sold		73,445
Gross profit		35,572
Operating expenses:		
Selling, general and administrative		22,635
Research and development		3,199
Depreciation		1,123
Operating income		8,615
Interest expense		805
Other (income)/expense, net		-87
Income before income taxes		7,897
Provision for income taxes		2,764
Net income	$	5,133

Figure 22

Generally, the best businesses spend fewer revenue dollars on these activities than their competitors. Some companies sell such a valuable product or service that they do not have to advertise much because customers do the selling through word of mouth. This is the best kind of advertising because it is free. If, on the other hand, a business is selling a product or service that is just average, and people do not really need it, a significant amount of resources needs to be spent convincing people to buy it.

RESEARCH AND DEVELOPMENT EXPENSES

Research and development expenses involve spending money to improve existing products or create new products. The amount of research and development expense varies based on the type of business. For example, Intel  has to spend significantly more on the research and development of new products than Wrigley, which produces chewing gum.

Income Statement

		31-Dec-11
Revenues	$	109,017
Cost of goods sold		73,445
Gross profit		35,572
Operating expenses:		
Selling, general and administrative		22,635
Research and development		3,199
Depreciation		1,123
Operating income		8,615
Interest expense		805
Other (income)/expense, net		-87
Income before income taxes		7,897
Provision for income taxes		2,764
Net income	$	5,133

Figure 23

The amount of research and development expense can give companies competitive advantages. Because Microsoft is a huge and successful company, it can spend billions of dollars on this activity without a problem and thus position itself in the marketplace to make even more money. A small start-up may be lucky to be able to spend a million dollars a year on research and development activities, never reaping the benefits that a giant like Microsoft can generate.

One negative aspect of research and development spending is that companies in certain industries have to spend more on it than companies in other industries.

For example, if Apple stopped developing new products, it would no longer have viable products in the marketplace because electronics and technology products quickly become obsolete. On the other hand, a company like International Speedway Corporation does not have to spend money on research and development because hosting NASCAR races does not require constant innovation.

One can argue that it is less risky to buy stocks of companies that do not need to rely on huge research and development expenditures because there is always some other company that can make their products obsolete with a technological breakthrough.

DEPRECIATION

Depreciation is the gradual expenditure of fixed assets from the balance sheet onto the income statement. Because fixed assets last for more than a single year, only a portion of the cost is expensed yearly through depreciation. At first, when a fixed asset is acquired, it is recorded on the balance sheet under the property, plant and equipment account. Through depreciation, the fixed asset is gradually transferred from the balance sheet to the income statement as an expense.

Income Statement

		31-Dec-11
Revenues	$	109,017
Cost of goods sold		73,445
Gross profit		35,572
Operating expenses:		
Selling, general and administrative		22,635
Research and development		3,199
Depreciation		1,123
Operating income		8,615
Interest expense		805
Other (income)/expense, net		-87
Income before income taxes		7,897
Provision for income taxes		2,764
Net income	$	5,133

Figure 24

Depreciation is considered a non-cash expense because the money required to purchase a particular fixed asset has already been spent. As a result, some investors treat depreciation as if it were not an expense by adding it back to operating income. For example, they use a metric called EBITDA (Earnings Before Interest, Taxes, Depreciation and Amortization) to analyze the earning power of a company and compare it to its competitors. This kind of thinking is flawed. There would not have been much earning power had it not been for the fixed assets. Cash was spent to purchase these fixed assets for a purpose – it was spent to put these assets to work and generate money. Therefore, depreciation is a real expense and should be treated as such. No one is adding back the cost of goods sold because it was spent in the past. Just as the cost of goods sold is matched against the corresponding revenue under accrual based accounting, depreciation is matched against revenue; however, the difference is that fixed assets last for many years and are expensed through depreciation gradually over their expected life span.

Companies that require huge amounts of fixed assets have high depreciation expenses. For example, auto manufacturers and airline companies have more fixed assets to depreciate than retail stores. Therefore, comparing the depreciation expenses of companies in different industries does not yield meaningful conclusions. A better comparison would be made between competitors operating in the same industry. Stronger players with dominant market positions can use their fixed asset base more efficiently by being able to produce greater revenue streams out of those assets as compared to weaker players. As a result, the depreciation expense as a percentage of revenues tends to be lower for stronger players.

OPERATING INCOME

Operating income is achieved after all of the operating expenses are subtracted from the gross profit. It does not include non-operating income and expenses, such as income from dividends and interest expense. Operating income is a profitability measure that is also referred to as EBIT, which stands for earnings before interest and taxes.

Income Statement

		31-Dec-11
Revenues	$	109,017
Cost of goods sold		73,445
Gross profit		35,572
Operating expenses:		
Selling, general and administrative		22,635
Research and development		3,199
Depreciation		1,123
Operating income		8,615
Interest expense		805
Other (income)/expense, net		-87
Income before income taxes		7,897
Provision for income taxes		2,764
Net income	$	5,133

Figure 25

INTEREST EXPENSE

The operating income only shows the earning power of a company as if it owned all of its assets free and clear. However, this view is flawed because businesses borrow money to finance portions of their assets, and, as a result, they are required to pay interest – the cost of money. Because interest is considered a financial cost, it is reported in the non-operating section below the operating income, as shown in Figure 26.

Income Statement

		31-Dec-11
Revenues	$	109,017
Cost of goods sold		73,445
Gross profit		35,572
Operating expenses:		
Selling, general and administrative		22,635
Research and development		3,199
Depreciation		1,123
Operating income		8,615
Interest expense		805
Other (income)/expense, net		-87
Income before income taxes		7,897
Provision for income taxes		2,764
Net income	$	5,133

Figure 26

The amount of interest expense is directly correlated with the amount of debt. Some companies tend to have lower or no interest expenses when they are so profitable that they can finance the majority their assets and operations internally. Companies that have to borrow because their operations are not profitable enough might not be in good shape unless, of course, they are still in the beginning stages where they have not yet reached profitability. It is not unusual to encounter companies that show positive operating income before interest expenses are subtracted but are clearly losing money after interest expenses are taken into account.

OTHER INCOME AND EXPENSES

Other income and expenses result from sources not related to operating activities. Examples of such items include interest income on cash balances at the bank, gains and losses from asset sales, and other nonrecurring items. The negative number shown in Figure 27 represents income of $87 that helps to offset the interest expense of $805.

Income Statement

		31-Dec-11
Revenues	$	109,017
Cost of goods sold		73,445
Gross profit		35,572
Operating expenses:		
Selling, general and administrative		22,635
Research and development		3,199
Depreciation		1,123
Operating income		8,615
Interest expense		805
Other (income)/expense, net		-87
Income before income taxes		7,897
Provision for income taxes		2,764
Net income	$	5,133

Figure 27

In the next chapter, which covers the cash flow statement, items, such as gains and losses from asset sales, that are included in the non-operating section of the income statement are taken out of the operating section of the cash flow statement and reclassified into other sections of the cash flow statement. This concept will become clearer in the next chapter.

PROVISION FOR INCOME TAXES

Provision for income taxes is an estimate of the company's tax expense for a given period of time. It is not the actual payment of taxes; it is an estimated amount of money set aside to pay this expense in the future.

Income Statement

		31-Dec-11
Revenues	$	109,017
Cost of goods sold		73,445
Gross profit		35,572
Operating expenses:		
Selling, general and administrative		22,635
Research and development		3,199
Depreciation		1,123
Operating income		8,615
Interest expense		805
Other (income)/expense, net		-87
Income before income taxes		7,897
Provision for income taxes		2,764
Net income	$	5,133

Figure 28

NET INCOME

Net income is the bottom line that is achieved after all the operating expenses, non-operating expenses, and income taxes are subtracted from the revenues. This is the measure of the company's profitability.

Income Statement

		31-Dec-11
Revenues	$	109,017
Cost of goods sold		73,445
Gross profit		35,572
Operating expenses:		
Selling, general and administrative		22,635
Research and development		3,199
Depreciation		1,123
Operating income		8,615
Interest expense		805
Other (income)/expense, net		-87
Income before income taxes		7,897
Provision for income taxes		2,764
Net income	$	5,133

Figure 29

A company that consistently shows an upward trend in net income from one year to another is most likely reinvesting its earnings back into its operations by adding more assets, acquiring other businesses, and paying down debt. Net income is used in the calculation of the net profit margin by dividing it by total revenues.

NET PROFIT MARGIN=NET INCOME/REVENUES

By using the numbers from Figure 29, we arrive at the following net profit margin.

NET PROFIT MARGIN = 5,133 / 109,017 = 4.71%

Similar to the gross profit margin, the net profit margin can be used for side-by-side comparisons between the subject company and its competitors. In the majority of cases, an enterprise that consistently outperforms its competitors in terms of net profit margin may have some type of competitive advantage because it can either charge more for its products or control its cost structure better.

Net income is also used in calculating return on equity, which shows the company's profitability in relation to the investment made in the shareholders' equity. Unlike net profit margin, calculating return on equity requires both the income statement and balance sheet as shown in the following formula:

RETURN ON EQUITY

=

NET INCOME/SHAREHOLDERS' EQUITY

By using the numbers from Figure 1 (Balance Sheet) and Figure 29, we arrive at the following return on equity.

RETURN ON EQUITY= 5,133 / 63,680 = 8.06%

Return on equity (ROE) can also be used to make side-by-side comparisons between competitors. Companies that generate a higher return on equity than their competitors tend to possess some type of competitive advantage that allows them to generate above average profits in relation to the shareholders' equity.

EARNINGS PER SHARE (EPS)

Earnings per share (EPS) is nothing more than net income distributed equally to all the available shares. It is reported below net income as shown in Figure 30.

Income Statement

		31-Dec-11
Revenues	$	109,017
Cost of goods sold		73,445
Gross profit		35,572
Operating expenses:		
Selling, general and administrative		22,635
Research and development		3,199
Depreciation		1,123
Operating income		8,615
Interest expense		805
Other (income)/expense, net		-87
Income before income taxes		7,897
Provision for income taxes		2,764
Net income	$	5,133
Basic earnings per share	$	0.82
Diluted earnings per share	$	0.81
Weighted average shares outstanding:		
Basic		6,286
Diluted		6,343

Figure 30

Earnings per share (EPS) equals net income divided by the number of shares outstanding. However, there are two entries for earnings per share – basic and diluted.

Earnings Per Share Calculation

Basic EPS	=	**Net Income / Basic Shares Outstanding**
	=	$5,133 / 6,286
	=	$0.82

Diluted EPS	=	**Net Income / Diluted Shares Outstanding**
	=	$5,133 / 6,343
	=	$0.81

Figure 31

Basic earnings per share are calculated based on the basic shares outstanding (6,286 in the example in Figure 30), and diluted earnings per share are calculated based on the diluted shares outstanding (6,343 in the example in Figure 30). Basic shares outstanding represent the total shares issued by the company that are still outstanding (this line item does not include repurchased shares).

Diluted shares outstanding include basic shares outstanding adjusted for the possibility of all convertible securities to be converted into common stock. Examples of convertible securities are stock options, warrants, and convertible preferred shares.

To be conservative, it is advisable to place more emphasis on the diluted earnings per share than the basic earnings per share. While in the previous example, the difference between the two is insignificant ($0.01 per share), in other instances, such as in high-tech companies that issue a significant number of stock options, the gap between the two measures of earnings per share can be larger.

Even though earnings per share are calculated based on net income, they can be trending up or down at different rates than net income. For example, if the net income of a particular company is increasing at five percent per year, the management can accelerate the growth in earnings per share by repurchasing the company's shares thereby, reducing the number of shares used in their calculation.

SUMMARY

Net income and earnings per share are very important in the investment world. Actually, Wall Street is obsessed with them. When a company reports better-than-expected earnings per share, its stock price is likely to increase and vice versa. Although both of these measures of profitability are important, they should not be solely relied upon because of the nature of accrual basis accounting. Profits are very important, but they are not the same as cash, and cash is what is used to purchase more equipment, acquire other businesses, reduce debt, and pay dividends. Net income and earnings per share can be smoothed out by the management. For example, reserves for bad debts and other reserve accounts are based on historical data, and also on estimates and the management's judgment. They can therefore be inflated when companies can afford to keep earnings out of the income statement and still beat earnings expectations in order to be used during lean quarters to continue to appear to meet those expectations. In addition, the management might have the financial incentive to manipulate those earnings to increase their company's stock price, thus increasing the prices of the managers' stock options. For these reasons, it is important that investors understand how to read the cash flow statement, which is the focus of the next chapter.

Cash Flow
Statement

Chapter 3

Cash Flow Statement

Companies can either use cash or accrual basis accounting, but firms that want to be publicly traded in the U.S. are required to follow GAAP, which is synonymous with accrual basis accounting. However, the movement of actual cash is very important for investors to understand. The statement of cash flows reconciles net income under GAAP rules into the change in the cash balance through various adjustments. If all companies used cash basis accounting, there would be no use for the cash flow statement because it would be identical to the income statement, and thus would be redundant. The cash flow statement, like the income statement, is prepared for a set period of time, such as a quarter or a year. The income statement shows the company's profitability, whereas the cash flow statement records the movement of cash through various sources and uses of cash. A sample cash flow statement is shown in Figure 32.

Cash Flow Statement

		2011
Operating Activities		
Net income	$	8,732
Adjustments to reconcile net income to net cash		
provided by operating activities:		
Depreciation expense		2,123
Gain/loss on sale of fixed assets		89
Changes in operating assets and liabilities:		
Accounts receivable		2,312
Inventories		-1,100
Prepaid expenses and other current assets		110
Accounts payable		1,068
Accrued expenses		-987
Income taxes payable		-60
Net cash provided by operating activities	$	12,287
Investing Activities		
Capital expenditures		-3,541
Business acquisitions		-2,000
Purchase/sale of equity investments		1,400
Purchase/sale of short-term investments		-1,100
Net cash used in investing activities	$	-5,241
Financing Activities		
Borrowing/repayment of long-term debt		-3,389
Issuance of common stock		0
Stock repurchases		-2,000
Cash dividends paid		-3,000
Net cash (used in) provided by financing activities	$	-8,389
Net (decrease) increase in cash and cash equivalents		-1,343
Cash and cash equivalents at beginning of year		4,273
Cash and cash equivalents at end of year	$	2,930

Figure 32

Sources of cash include transactions such as selling products, borrowing from banks, issuing shares, and collecting accounts receivable. The uses of cash include paying suppliers, repaying lenders, repurchasing shares, and paying dividends.

Before discussing different sections of the cash flow statement, it is beneficial to go to the bottom of the statement where cash and cash equivalents are recorded for the beginning and end of a reporting period. These same amounts are also recorded on the balance sheet as shown in the following illustration:

Cash Flow Statement

	2011
Operating Activities	
Net income	$ 8,732
Adjustments to reconcile net income to net cash provided by operating activities:	
Depreciation expense	2,123
Gain/loss on sale of fixed assets	89
Changes in operating assets and liabilities:	
Accounts receivable	2,312
Inventories	-1,100
Prepaid expenses and other current assets	110
Accounts payable	1,068
Accrued expenses	-987
Income taxes payable	-60
Net cash provided by operating activities	$ 12,287
Investing Activities	
Capital expenditures	-3,541
Business acquisitions	-2,000
Purchase/sale of equity investments	1,400
Purchase/sale of short-term investments	-1,100
Net cash used in investing activities	$ -5,241
Financing Activities	
Borrowing/repayment of long-term debt	-3,389
Issuance of common stock	0
Stock repurchases	-2,000
Cash dividends paid	-3,000
Net cash (used in) provided by financing activities	$ -8,389
Net (decrease) increase in cash and cash equivalents	-1,343
Cash and cash equivalents at beginning of year	4,273
Cash and cash equivalents at end of year	$ 2,930

Balance Sheet

	2010	2011	Change
Assets			
Current Assets			
Cash and cash equivalents	$ 4,273	2,930	-1,343
Accounts receivable	X,XXX	X,XXX	
Inventories	X,XXX	X,XXX	
Prepaid expenses	X,XXX	X,XXX	
Total current assets	X,XXX	X,XXX	
Property, plant and equipment, net	X,XXX	X,XXX	
Other assets	X,XXX	X,XXX	
Total assets	$ X,XXX	X,XXX	
Liabilities and Shareholders' Equity			
Current liabilities			
Accounts payable	$ X,XXX	X,XXX	
Accrued expenses	X,XXX	X,XXX	
Current portion of long-term debt	X,XXX	X,XXX	
Income taxes payable	X,XXX	X,XXX	
Total current liabilities	X,XXX	X,XXX	
Long-term debt	X,XXX	X,XXX	
Total liabilities	X,XXX	X,XXX	
Shareholders' equity:			
Capital Stock	X,XXX	X,XXX	
Additional paid-in capital	X,XXX	X,XXX	
Retained earnings	X,XXX	X,XXX	
Total shareholders' equity	X,XXX	X,XXX	
Total liabilities and shareholders' equity	$ X,XXX	X,XXX	

Figure 33

In the cash flow statement in Figure 33, the cash balance at the beginning of year was $4,273 and at the end of the year it was $2,930. This means that it decreased by $1,343 during the year. All the cash flow statement does is explain how the cash balance went from one amount at the beginning of the year to another amount at the end of the year or other reporting period. The following are some of the questions that the cash flow statement answers:

- What were the sources of cash?
- Did the majority of cash come from operations or from the sale of fixed assets?
- Did the company borrow money or issue more shares to increase the cash level?
- How did the company spend its extra cash after all the operational bills were paid?
- Did it invest in new equipment, repurchase shares, or pay dividends?

At the bottom of the cash flow statement, the change in the cash and cash equivalents balance during the reporting period is shown by the net (decrease) increase in cash and cash equivalents, which is calculated by combining the cash flows from the three categories on the cash flow statement. In Figure 34, there is a net decrease in cash of $1,343.

The Basics of Understanding Financial Statements

Cash Flow Statement

	2011
Operating Activities	
Net income	$ 8,732
Adjustments to reconcile net income to net cash	
provided by operating activities:	
Depreciation expense	2,123
Gain/loss on sale of fixed assets	89
Changes in operating assets and liabilities:	
Accounts receivable	2,312
Inventories	-1,100
Prepaid expenses and other current assets	110
Accounts payable	1,068
Accrued expenses	-987
Income taxes payable	-60
Net cash provided by operating activities	$ 12,287
Investing Activities	
Capital expenditures	-3,541
Business acquisitions	-2,000
Purchase/sale of equity investments	1,400
Purchase/sale of short-term investments	-1,100
Net cash used in investing activities	$ -5,241
Financing Activities	
Borrowing/repayment of long-term debt	-3,389
Issuance of common stock	0
Stock repurchases	-2,000
Cash dividends paid	-3,000
Net cash (used in) provided by financing activities	$ -8,389
Net (decrease) increase in cash and cash equivalents	-1,343
Cash and cash equivalents at beginning of year	4,273
Cash and cash equivalents at end of year	$ 2,930

$12,287
+
-$5,241
+
-$8,389
=
-$1,343

Figure 34

The cash flow statement is classified into three categories: cash provided or used by 1) operating activities, 2) investing activities, and 3) financing activities as shown in Figure 35.

Cash Flow Statement

	2011
Operating Activities	
Net income	$ 8,732
Adjustments to reconcile net income to net cash provided by operating activities:	
Depreciation expense	2,123
Gain/loss on sale of fixed assets	89
Changes in operating assets and liabilities:	
Accounts receivable	2,312
Inventories	-1,100
Prepaid expenses and other current assets	110
Accounts payable	1,068
Accrued expenses	-987
Income taxes payable	-60
Net cash provided by operating activities	$ 12,287
Investing Activities	
Capital expenditures	-3,541
Business acquisitions	-2,000
Purchase/sale of equity investments	1,400
Purchase/sale of short-term investments	-1,100
Net cash used in investing activities	$ -5,241
Financing Activities	
Borrowing/repayment of long-term debt	-3,389
Issuance of common stock	0
Stock repurchases	-2,000
Cash dividends paid	-3,000
Net cash (used in) provided by financing activities	$ -8,389
Net (decrease) increase in cash and cash equivalents	-1,343
Cash and cash equivalents at beginning of year	4,273
Cash and cash equivalents at end of year	$ 2,930

Figure 35

OPERATING ACTIVITIES

Cash provided by operating activities involves the cash effects of transactions that occurred to allow the realization of net income on the income statement. Cash flows in this category include cash receipts from customers from the sales of goods and services and from interest and dividends received from loans and investments. Cash outflows are cash payments to pay for supplies, labor, operating expenses, interest, and taxes.

To arrive at net cash provided by operating activities, the cash flow statement starts with net income, followed by several adjustments that are made to it.

Cash Flow Statement

	2011
Operating Activities	
Net income	$ 8,732
Adjustments to reconcile net income to net cash provided by operating activities:	
Depreciation expense	2,123
Gain/loss on sale of fixed assets	89
Changes in operating assets and liabilities:	
Accounts receivable	2,312
Inventories	-1,100
Prepaid expenses and other current assets	110
Accounts payable	1,068
Accrued expenses	-987
Income taxes payable	-60
Net cash provided by operating activities	$ 12,287

Figure 36

DEPRECIATION EXPENSE ADJUSTMENT

The depreciation expense is usually the first adjustment that is made to net income. As mentioned before, depreciation is the gradual transfer of fixed assets from the balance sheet onto the income statement due to the use of the assets and the passage of time. Because the depreciation expense reduces net income but is a non-cash transaction, it must be added back to net income to calculate net cash provided by operating activities.

Cash Flow Statement

	2011
Operating Activities	
Net income	8,732
Adjustments to reconcile net income to net cash provided by operating activities:	
Depreciation expense	2,123
Gain/loss on sale of fixed assets	89
Changes in operating assets and liabilities:	
Accounts receivable	2,312
Inventories	-1,100
Prepaid expenses and other current assets	110
Accounts payable	1,068
Accrued expenses	-987
Income taxes payable	-60
Net cash provided by operating activities	12,287

Income Statement

	2011
Revenues	X,XXX
Cost of goods sold	X,XXX
Gross profit	X,XXX
Operating expenses:	
Selling, general and administrative	X,XXX
Research and development	X,XXX
Depreciation	2,123
Operating income	X,XXX
Interest expense	X,XXX
Other (income)/expense, net	X,XXX
Income before income taxes	X,XXX
Provision for income taxes	X,XXX
Net income	X,XXX

Figure 37

The cash flow statement must represent when cash was paid for the fixed assets, whether all cash was paid in the same period or over several quarters or years. This is reflected in the investing activities section, which is discussed later.

GAIN/LOSS ON SALE OF FIXED ASSETS ADJUSTMENT

When companies choose to sell some of their fixed assets, this may result either in a gain or loss included in net income. Because the sale of a fixed asset is not considered a regular operating activity, it should not be included in the determination of cash provided by operating activities. Therefore, the gain or loss must be removed from the operating activities section and be reflected in the investing activities section. Hence, any gain needs to be subtracted and any loss added to adjust net income in the operating activities section. Gains and losses from the sales of fixed assets will be reflected in the investing section within the capital expenditures figure.

Cash Flow Statement

	2011
Operating Activities	
Net income	8,732
Adjustments to reconcile net income to net cash provided by operating activities:	
Depreciation expense	2,123
Gain/loss on sale of fixed assets	89
Changes in operating assets and liabilities:	
Accounts receivable	2,312
Inventories	-1,100
Prepaid expenses and other current assets	110
Accounts payable	1,068
Accrued expenses	-987
Income taxes payable	-60
Net cash provided by operating activities	12,287

Income Statement

	2011
Revenues	X,XXX
Cost of goods sold	X,XXX
Gross profit	X,XXX
Operating expenses:	
Selling, general and administrative	X,XXX
Research and development	X,XXX
Depreciation	X,XXX
Operating income	X,XXX
Interest expense	X,XXX
Other (income)/expense, net	89
Income before income taxes	X,XXX
Provision for income taxes	X,XXX
Net income	X,XXX

Figure 38

CHANGES IN OPERATING ASSETS AND LIABILITIES

There are transactions that do not affect net income (they only affect balance sheet accounts), but do affect the cash flow statement. Such transactions are changes in operating assets and liabilities.

Cash Flow Statement

	2011
Operating Activities	
Net income	$ 8,732
Adjustments to reconcile net income to net cash provided by operating activities:	
Depreciation expense	2,123
Gain/loss on sale of fixed assets	89
Changes in operating assets and liabilities:	
Accounts receivable	2,312
Inventories	-1,100
Prepaid expenses and other current assets	110
Accounts payable	1,068
Accrued expenses	-987
Income taxes payable	-60
Net cash provided by operating activities	$ 12,287

Figure 39

An increase in asset accounts represents a net expenditure of cash to acquire those assets. Since this extra cash outflow is not reflected in net income, a negative adjustment to net income must be made in order to reconcile it to the change in the cash account. Alternatively, a decrease in asset accounts reflects the net freeing up of cash not reflected in net income, and it would necessitate a positive adjustment to net income on the cash flow statement.

A decrease in liability accounts (amounts owed to others) represents extra cash expended in that period to pay them down. For example, if your credit card balance at the end of the month is lower than at the beginning of the month, it means you spent cash to pay it down. Since this extra cash outflow is not reflected in net income, a negative adjustment to net income must be made in order to reconcile it to the change in the cash account. On the other hand, an increase in liability accounts represents less cash paid to creditors (cash savings) not reflected in net income, and therefore, would necessitate a positive adjustment to net income on the cash flow statement.

Transactions that affect current assets and liabilities accounts occur during the regular conduct of business; hence, changes to these accounts from one period to the next must be reflected as adjustments in the operating section of the cash flow statement.

ACCOUNTS RECEIVABLE ADJUSTMENT

On the balance sheet in Figure 40, the accounts receivable account decreased from $9,825 at the end of 2010 to $7,513 at the end of 2011, which is a $2,312 decrease. Therefore, the company's customers paid down their credit obligations and thus, provided the company with a cash inflow that is not reflected in net income. Therefore, a positive adjustment is made to net income on the cash flow statement.

Cash Flow Statement

	2011
Operating Activities	
Net income	$ 8,732
Adjustments to reconcile net income to net cash provided by operating activities:	
Depreciation expense	2,123
Gain/loss on sale of fixed assets	89
Changes in operating assets and liabilities:	
Accounts receivable	2,312
Inventories	-1,100
Prepaid expenses and other current assets	110
Accounts payable	1,068
Accrued expenses	-987
Income taxes payable	-60
Net cash provided by operating activities	$ 12,287
Investing Activities	
Capital expenditures	-3,541
Business acquisitions	-2,000
Purchase/sale of equity investments	1,400
Purchase/sale of short-term investments	-1,100
Net cash used in investing activities	$ -5,241
Financing Activities	
Borrowing/repayment of long-term debt	-3,389
Issuance of common stock	0
Stock repurchases	-2,000
Cash dividends paid	-3,000
Net cash (used in) provided by financing activities	$ -8,389
Net (decrease) increase in cash and cash equivalents	-1,343
Cash and cash equivalents at beginning of year	4,273
Cash and cash equivalents at end of year	$ 2,930

Balance Sheet

	2010	2011	Change
Assets			
Current Assets			
Cash and cash equivalents	$ X,XXX	X,XXX	
Accounts receivable	9,825	7,513	-2,312
Inventories	X,XXX	X,XXX	
Prepaid expenses	X,XXX	X,XXX	
Total current assets	X,XXX	X,XXX	
Property, plant and equipment, net	X,XXX	X,XXX	
Other assets	X,XXX	X,XXX	
Total assets	$ X,XXX	X,XXX	
Liabilities and Shareholders' Equity			
Current liabilities			
Accounts payable	$ X,XXX	X,XXX	
Accrued expenses	X,XXX	X,XXX	
Current portion of long-term debt	X,XXX	X,XXX	
Income taxes payable	X,XXX	X,XXX	
Total current liabilities	X,XXX	X,XXX	
Long-term debt	X,XXX	X,XXX	
Total liabilities	X,XXX	X,XXX	
Shareholders' equity:			
Capital Stock	X,XXX	X,XXX	
Additional paid-in capital	X,XXX	X,XXX	
Retained earnings	X,XXX	X,XXX	
Total shareholders' equity	X,XXX	X,XXX	
Total liabilities and shareholders' equity	$ X,XXX	X,XXX	

Figure 40

An increase in accounts receivable on the balance sheet would mean that less cash was received from customers, and a negative adjustment would be required to net income on the cash flow statement.

INVENTORY ADJUSTMENT

On the balance sheet in Figure 41, the inventory account increased from $9,900 at the end of 2010 to $11,000 at the end of 2011, which is a $1,100 increase. The company had to spend extra cash to purchase additional inventory, thereby increasing cash outflow that is not reflected in net income. Therefore, a negative adjustment is made to net income on the cash flow statement.

Cash Flow Statement

	2011
Operating Activities	
Net income	$ 8,732
Adjustments to reconcile net income to net cash provided by operating activities:	
Depreciation expense	2,123
Gain/loss on sale of fixed assets	89
Changes in operating assets and liabilities:	
Accounts receivable	2,312
Inventories	-1,100
Prepaid expenses and other current assets	110
Accounts payable	1,068
Accrued expenses	-987
Income taxes payable	-60
Net cash provided by operating activities	$ 12,287
Investing Activities	
Capital expenditures	-3,541
Business acquisitions	-2,000
Purchase/sale of equity investments	1,400
Purchase/sale of short-term investments	-1,100
Net cash used in investing activities	$ -5,241
Financing Activities	
Borrowing/repayment of long-term debt	-3,389
Issuance of common stock	0
Stock repurchases	-2,000
Cash dividends paid	-3,000
Net cash (used in) provided by financing activities	$ -8,389
Net (decrease) increase in cash and cash equivalents	-1,343
Cash and cash equivalents at beginning of year	4,273
Cash and cash equivalents at end of year	$ 2,930

Balance Sheet

	2010	2011	Change
Assets			
Current Assets			
Cash and cash equivalents	$ X,XXX	X,XXX	
Accounts receivable	X,XXX	X,XXX	
Inventories	9,900	11,000	1,100
Prepaid expenses	X,XXX	X,XXX	
Total current assets	X,XXX	X,XXX	
Property, plant and equipment, net	X,XXX	X,XXX	
Other assets	X,XXX	X,XXX	
Total assets	$ X,XXX	X,XXX	
Liabilities and Shareholders' Equity			
Current liabilities			
Accounts payable	$ X,XXX	X,XXX	
Accrued expenses	X,XXX	X,XXX	
Current portion of long-term debt	X,XXX	X,XXX	
Income taxes payable	X,XXX	X,XXX	
Total current liabilities	X,XXX	X,XXX	
Long-term debt	X,XXX	X,XXX	
Total liabilities	X,XXX	X,XXX	
Shareholders' equity:			
Capital Stock	X,XXX	X,XXX	
Additional paid-in capital	X,XXX	X,XXX	
Retained earnings	X,XXX	X,XXX	
Total shareholders' equity	X,XXX	X,XXX	
Total liabilities and shareholders' equity	$ X,XXX	X,XXX	

Figure 41

Had inventory decreased, it would mean that the company did not spend as much cash (cash savings) to purchase inventory, effectively, cash inflow that is not reflected in net income. This would have required a positive adjustment to net income on the cash flow statement.

PREPAID EXPENSE ADJUSTMENT

On the balance sheet in Figure 42, the prepaid expense account decreased from $1,244 at the end of 2010 to $1,134 at the end of 2011, which is a $110 decrease. The company used up more of its prepaid services than it paid out, which is a cash savings not reflected in net income. Therefore, a positive adjustment is made to net income on the cash flow statement.

Cash Flow Statement

	2011
Operating Activities	
Net income	$ 8,732
Adjustments to reconcile net income to net cash provided by operating activities:	
Depreciation expense	2,123
Gain/loss on sale of fixed assets	89
Changes in operating assets and liabilities:	
Accounts receivable	2,312
Inventories	-1,100
Prepaid expenses and other current assets	110
Accounts payable	1,068
Accrued expenses	-987
Income taxes payable	-60
Net cash provided by operating activities	$ 12,287
Investing Activities	
Capital expenditures	-3,541
Business acquisitions	-2,000
Purchase/sale of equity investments	1,400
Purchase/sale of short-term investments	-1,100
Net cash used in investing activities	$ -5,241
Financing Activities	
Borrowing/repayment of long-term debt	-3,389
Issuance of common stock	0
Stock repurchases	-2,000
Cash dividends paid	-3,000
Net cash (used in) provided by financing activities	$ -8,389
Net (decrease) increase in cash and cash equivalents	-1,343
Cash and cash equivalents at beginning of year	4,273
Cash and cash equivalents at end of year	$ 2,930

Balance Sheet

	2010	2011	Change
Assets			
Current Assets			
Cash and cash equivalents	$ X,XXX	X,XXX	
Accounts receivable	X,XXX	X,XXX	
Inventories	X,XXX	X,XXX	
Prepaid expenses	1,244	1,134	-110
Total current assets	X,XXX	X,XXX	
Property, plant and equipment, net	X,XXX	X,XXX	
Other assets	X,XXX	X,XXX	
Total assets	$ X,XXX	X,XXX	
Liabilities and Shareholders' Equity			
Current liabilities			
Accounts payable	$ X,XXX	X,XXX	
Accrued expenses	X,XXX	X,XXX	
Current portion of long-term debt	X,XXX	X,XXX	
Income taxes payable	X,XXX	X,XXX	
Total current liabilities	X,XXX	X,XXX	
Long-term debt	X,XXX	X,XXX	
Total liabilities	X,XXX	X,XXX	
Shareholders' equity:			
Capital Stock	X,XXX	X,XXX	
Additional paid-in capital	X,XXX	X,XXX	
Retained earnings	X,XXX	X,XXX	
Total shareholders' equity	X,XXX	X,XXX	
Total liabilities and shareholders' equity	$ X,XXX	X,XXX	

Figure 42

Had prepaid expenses increased, it would mean that cash left the company to prepay those future services, which is an extra cash outflow not reflected in net income. A negative adjustment would be required to net income on the cash flow statement.

ACCOUNTS PAYABLE ADJUSTMENT

On the balance sheet in Figure 43, the accounts payable account increased from $8,724 at the end of 2010 to $9,792 at the end of 2011, which is a $1,068 increase. This increase represents less cash paid to suppliers, which is a cash savings not reflected in net income. Therefore, a positive adjustment is made to net income on the cash flow statement.

Cash Flow Statement

	2011
Operating Activities	
Net income	$ 8,732
Adjustments to reconcile net income to net cash provided by operating activities:	
Depreciation expense	2,123
Gain/loss on sale of fixed assets	89
Changes in operating assets and liabilities:	
Accounts receivable	2,312
Inventories	-1,100
Prepaid expenses and other current assets	110
Accounts payable	1,068
Accrued expenses	-987
Income taxes payable	-60
Net cash provided by operating activities	$ 12,287
Investing Activities	
Capital expenditures	-3,541
Business acquisitions	-2,000
Purchase/sale of equity investments	1,400
Purchase/sale of short-term investments	-1,100
Net cash used in investing activities	$ -5,241
Financing Activities	
Borrowing/repayment of long-term debt	-3,389
Issuance of common stock	0
Stock repurchases	-2,000
Cash dividends paid	-3,000
Net cash (used in) provided by financing activities	$ -8,389
Net (decrease) increase in cash and cash equivalents	-1,343
Cash and cash equivalents at beginning of year	4,273
Cash and cash equivalents at end of year	$ 2,930

Balance Sheet

	2010	2011	Change
Assets			
Current Assets			
Cash and cash equivalents	$ X,XXX	X,XXX	
Accounts receivable	X,XXX	X,XXX	
Inventories	X,XXX	X,XXX	
Prepaid expenses	X,XXX	X,XXX	
Total current assets	X,XXX	X,XXX	
Property, plant and equipment, net	X,XXX	X,XXX	
Other assets	X,XXX	X,XXX	
Total assets	$ X,XXX	X,XXX	
Liabilities and Shareholders' Equity			
Current liabilities			
Accounts payable	$ 8,724	9,792	1,068
Accrued expenses	X,XXX	X,XXX	
Current portion of long-term debt	X,XXX	X,XXX	
Income taxes payable	X,XXX	X,XXX	
Total current liabilities	X,XXX	X,XXX	
Long-term debt	X,XXX	X,XXX	
Total liabilities	X,XXX	X,XXX	
Shareholders' equity:			
Capital Stock	X,XXX	X,XXX	
Additional paid-in capital	X,XXX	X,XXX	
Retained earnings	X,XXX	X,XXX	
Total shareholders' equity	X,XXX	X,XXX	
Total liabilities and shareholders' equity	$ X,XXX	X,XXX	

Figure 43

Had accounts payable decreased, it would mean that cash left the company to pay down the company's obligation to suppliers. This extra cash outflow is not reflected in net income, and therefore, a negative adjustment would be required to net income on the cash flow statement.

ACCRUED EXPENSES ADJUSTMENT

On the balance sheet in Figure 44, the accrued expense account decreased from $7,543 at the end of 2010 to $6,556 at the end of 2011, which is a $987 decrease. This decrease would mean that extra cash left the company to pay down the company's obligation to providers of services. This extra cash outflow is not reflected in net income, and therefore, a negative adjustment would be required to net income on the cash flow statement.

Cash Flow Statement

	2011
Operating Activities	
Net income	$ 8,732
Adjustments to reconcile net income to net cash provided by operating activities:	
Depreciation expense	2,123
Gain/loss on sale of fixed assets	89
Changes in operating assets and liabilities:	
Accounts receivable	2,312
Inventories	-1,100
Prepaid expenses and other current assets	110
Accounts payable	1,068
Accrued expenses	-987
Income taxes payable	-60
Net cash provided by operating activities	$ 12,287
Investing Activities	
Capital expenditures	-3,541
Business acquisitions	-2,000
Purchase/sale of equity investments	1,400
Purchase/sale of short-term investments	-1,100
Net cash used in investing activities	$ -5,241
Financing Activities	
Borrowing/repayment of long-term debt	-3,389
Issuance of common stock	0
Stock repurchases	-2,000
Cash dividends paid	-3,000
Net cash (used in) provided by financing activities	$ -8,389
Net (decrease) increase in cash and cash equivalents	-1,343
Cash and cash equivalents at beginning of year	4,273
Cash and cash equivalents at end of year	$ 2,930

Balance Sheet

	2010	2011	Change
Assets			
Current Assets			
Cash and cash equivalents	$ X,XXX	X,XXX	
Accounts receivable	X,XXX	X,XXX	
Inventories	X,XXX	X,XXX	
Prepaid expenses	X,XXX	X,XXX	
Total current assets	X,XXX	X,XXX	
Property, plant and equipment, net	X,XXX	X,XXX	
Other assets	X,XXX	X,XXX	
Total assets	$ X,XXX	X,XXX	
Liabilities and Shareholders' Equity			
Current liabilities			
Accounts payable	$ X,XXX	X,XXX	
Accrued expenses	7,543	6,556	-987
Current portion of long-term debt	X,XXX	X,XXX	
Income taxes payable	X,XXX	X,XXX	
Total current liabilities	X,XXX	X,XXX	
Long-term debt	X,XXX	X,XXX	
Total liabilities	X,XXX	X,XXX	
Shareholders' equity:			
Capital Stock	X,XXX	X,XXX	
Additional paid-in capital	X,XXX	X,XXX	
Retained earnings	X,XXX	X,XXX	
Total shareholders' equity	X,XXX	X,XXX	
Total liabilities and shareholders' equity	$ X,XXX	X,XXX	

Figure 44

Had accrued expenses increased, it would represent less cash paid to creditors, which is a cash savings not reflected in net income. Therefore, a positive adjustment would need to be made to net income on the cash flow statement.

INCOME TAXES PAYABLE ADJUSTMENT

On the balance sheet in Figure 45, the income taxes payable account decreased from $650 at the end of 2010 to $590 at the end of 2011, which is a $60 decrease. This decrease would mean that extra cash left the company to pay down the company's obligation to taxing authorities. This extra cash outflow is not reflected in net income, and therefore, a negative adjustment would be required to net income on the cash flow statement.

Cash Flow Statement

	2011
Operating Activities	
Net income	$ 8,732
Adjustments to reconcile net income to net cash	
provided by operating activities:	
Depreciation expense	2,123
Gain/loss on sale of fixed assets	89
Changes in operating assets and liabilities:	
Accounts receivable	2,312
Inventories	-1,100
Prepaid expenses and other current assets	110
Accounts payable	1,068
Accrued expenses	-987
Income taxes payable	-60
Net cash provided by operating activities	$ 12,287
Investing Activities	
Capital expenditures	-3,541
Business acquisitions	-2,000
Purchase/sale of equity investments	1,400
Purchase/sale of short-term investments	-1,100
Net cash used in investing activities	$ -5,241
Financing Activities	
Borrowing/repayment of long-term debt	-3,389
Issuance of common stock	0
Stock repurchases	-2,000
Cash dividends paid	-3,000
Net cash (used in) provided by financing activities	$ -8,389
Net (decrease) increase in cash and cash equivalents	-1,343
Cash and cash equivalents at beginning of year	4,273
Cash and cash equivalents at end of year	$ 2,930

Balance Sheet

	2010	2011	Change
Assets			
Current Assets			
Cash and cash equivalents	$ X,XXX	X,XXX	
Accounts receivable	X,XXX	X,XXX	
Inventories	X,XXX	X,XXX	
Prepaid expenses	X,XXX	X,XXX	
Total current assets	X,XXX	X,XXX	
Property, plant and equipment, net	X,XXX	X,XXX	
Other assets	X,XXX	X,XXX	
Total assets	$ X,XXX	X,XXX	
Liabilities and Shareholders' Equity			
Current liabilities			
Accounts payable	$ X,XXX	X,XXX	
Accrued expenses	X,XXX	X,XXX	
Current portion of long-term debt	X,XXX	X,XXX	
Income taxes payable	650	590	-60
Total current liabilities	X,XXX	X,XXX	
Long-term debt	X,XXX	X,XXX	
Total liabilities	X,XXX	X,XXX	
Shareholders' equity:			
Capital Stock	X,XXX	X,XXX	
Additional paid-in capital	X,XXX	X,XXX	
Retained earnings	X,XXX	X,XXX	
Total shareholders' equity	X,XXX	X,XXX	
Total liabilities and shareholders' equity	$ X,XXX	X,XXX	

Figure 45

Had income taxes payable increased, it would represent less cash paid to taxing authorities, which is a cash savings not reflected in net income. Therefore, a positive adjustment would need to be made to net income on the cash flow statement.

NET CASH PROVIDED BY OPERATING ACTIVITIES

After combining all the adjustments and applying them to net income, the resulting figure is net cash provided by operating activities. Because cash flow from operating activities is derived from renewable sources – operations – it is more valuable than cash coming from investing or financing activities. For example, the company might be shedding assets. This would create a positive investing cash flow, but it could not be sustained because, at some point, there would be no more assets to sell. The same principle applies to cash coming from financing activities. The company can borrow money to bring more cash in the door, but there is a limit on how much lenders will lend. A company that can continuously use operating cash flow to finance acquisitions of new fixed assets, payments of dividends, repayments of debt, and repurchases of shares is likely making its shareholders wealthy.

Cash Flow Statement

	2011
Operating Activities	
Net income	$ 8,732
Adjustments to reconcile net income to net cash provided by operating activities:	
Depreciation expense	2,123
Gain/loss on sale of fixed assets	89
Changes in operating assets and liabilities:	
Accounts receivable	2,312
Inventories	-1,100
Prepaid expenses and other current assets	110
Accounts payable	1,068
Accrued expenses	-987
Income taxes payable	-60
Net cash provided by operating activities	$ 12,287

Figure 46

INVESTING ACTIVITIES

Cash flows from investing activities involve the acquiring and disposing of fixed assets, other businesses, equity investments, and short-term investments. These transactions are not reflected in net income, but since they affect cash, they need to appear on the cash flow statement in Figure 47.

Cash Flow Statement

		2011
Operating Activities		
Net income	$	8,732
Adjustments to reconcile net income to net cash provided by operating activities:		
Depreciation expense		2,123
Gain/loss on sale of fixed assets		89
Changes in operating assets and liabilities:		
Accounts receivable		2,312
Inventories		-1,100
Prepaid expenses and other current assets		110
Accounts payable		1,068
Accrued expenses		-987
Income taxes payable		-60
Net cash provided by operating activities	$	12,287
Investing Activities		
Capital expenditures		-3,541
Business acquisitions		-2,000
Purchase/sale of equity investments		1,400
Purchase/sale of short-term investments		-1,100
Net cash used in investing activities	$	-5,241
Financing Activities		
Borrowing/repayment of long-term debt		-3,389
Issuance of common stock		0
Stock repurchases		-2,000
Cash dividends paid		-3,000
Net cash (used in) provided by financing activities	$	-8,389
Net (decrease) increase in cash and cash equivalents		-1,343
Cash and cash equivalents at beginning of year		4,273
Cash and cash equivalents at end of year	$	2,930

Figure 47

CAPITAL EXPENDITURES

Whenever fixed assets are purchased, they are recorded as cash outflow in the investing activities during the period of acquisition regardless of the asset's life span. Remember, on the income statement these same assets are depreciated slowly over many years. The purchases of property, plant and equipment are also referred to as capital expenditures.

Cash Flow Statement

	2011
Investing Activities	
Capital expenditures	-3,541
Business acquisitions	-2,000
Purchase/sale of equity investments	1,400
Purchase/sale of short-term investments	-1,100
Net cash used in investing activities	$ -5,241

Figure 48

Because of the previously mentioned limitations of net income and earnings per share, many investors turn to a different measure of the company's financial success – the free cash flow. There are several theories on how to calculate free cash flow, but for our purposes, we will use the following base formula:

FREE CASH FLOW
=
OPERATING CASH FLOW - CAPITAL EXPENDITURES

Free cash flow refers to the cash flow provided by operations after the maintenance of the firm's productive capacity. It is the cash flow that can be used to benefit shareholders through actions such as paying down debt, acquiring other companies, paying dividends, and repurchasing shares.

However, capital expenditures have to be analyzed in more detail because they include both the replacement and growth components of capital expenditures. Replacement capital expenditures are those that only maintain the firm's productivity; they do not increase it. Adding more fixed assets that allow the company to produce and serve more customers increases the company's earning power and generates growth. Replacement capital expenditures should be included in the calculation of free cash flow but growth capital expenditures should not. The adjusted formula for free cash flow is as follows:

FREE CASH FLOW
=
OPERATING CASH FLOW - REPLACEMENT CAPITAL EXPENDITURES

Inexperienced investors often misunderstand this concept. For example, some investors criticized International Speedway Corporation for having a negative free cash flow. If they understood the concept as it was just described, they would have realized that the reason why International Speedway Corporation appeared to have a negative free cash flow was because it was spending a significant amount of money to add seating capacity to its speedways in order to increase the company's earning power. Had they deducted only the replacement portion of these capital expenditures, they would have realized that the company generated positive free cash flow.

In order to separate capital expenditures into two components, investors need to read the company's annual reports, and, at times, consult the company's management.

BUSINESS ACQUISITIONS

The investing activities section allows investors to learn how much cash the company is spending on acquiring other businesses. Acquisitions of other businesses can be beneficial to shareholders if they are consistent with the company's strategy and are accomplished at the right price. Unfortunately, companies often overpay in the pursuit to expand their empires. To determine whether acquisitions are benefiting shareholders, investors need to learn more about each particular deal by reading the company's filings, listening to conference calls, and interviewing managers. Analyzing acquisitions is like analyzing investments. It is important to determine and compare the benefits and the costs of each particular acquisition. Since it is not apparent for years whether an acquisition was successful, it is useful to analyze previous acquisitions to assess the management's track record. Business acquisitions are recorded as cash outflows because cash is being spent, while dispositions of these businesses are recorded as cash inflows because cash is being received.

Cash Flow Statement

	2011
Investing Activities	
Capital expenditures	-3,541
Business acquisitions	-2,000
Purchase/sale of equity investments	1,400
Purchase/sale of short-term investments	-1,100
Net cash used in investing activities	$ -5,241

Figure 49

PURCHASE/SALE OF EQUITY INVESTMENTS

Aside from acquiring more fixed assets or other businesses, a company can also invest in common stocks. These transactions are included under investing activities. For example, if the CEO of a company decided to buy International Speedway Corporation for the company's account, this transaction would be recorded in the investing section of the cash flow statement. Acquisitions of equity investments are recorded as cash outflows because cash is being spent, while dispositions of equity investments are recorded as cash inflows because cash is being received.

Cash Flow Statement

	2011
Investing Activities	
Capital expenditures	-3,541
Business acquisitions	-2,000
Purchase/sale of equity investments	1,400
Purchase/sale of short-term investments	-1,100
Net cash used in investing activities	$ -5,241

Figure 50

The difference between business acquisitions and equity investments is based how much of the company is being acquired.

PURCHASE/SALE OF SHORT-TERM INVESTMENTS

Instead of sitting on cash, companies can park it in short-term investments. When the management is ready to put the company's capital to work in more beneficial ways, it can simply liquidate short-term investments and use the proceeds to buy more fixed assets and acquire other businesses. When short-term investments are liquidated, the cash flow effect is positive because cash is being received, and when they are acquired, it is negative because money is being spent.

Cash Flow Statement

	2011
Investing Activities	
Capital expenditures	-3,541
Business acquisitions	-2,000
Purchase/sale of equity investments	1,400
Purchase/sale of short-term investments	-1,100
Net cash used in investing activities	$ -5,241

Figure 51

It is the responsibility of the management to allocate capital in the way that benefits shareholders the most. It is acceptable for cash to be invested in short-term investments earning low returns until more productive uses for it are identified. However, if over a long period of time the management is unable to reinvest its cash at higher rates, it should return it to shareholders in the form of dividends or share buybacks.

NET CASH USED IN INVESTING ACTIVITIES

Combining all the cash inflows and outflows of investing activities results in net cash used in investing activities. When the company continuously generates positive net cash provided by operating activities, it will have excess cash that can be used to expand its business by acquiring more assets, other businesses, and various investments. In such instances, net cash used in investing activities is likely to be negative. However, if the company experiences a negative operating cash flow, yet shows a positive investing cash flow, this is not a good sign because it could mean that the company is liquidating its assets to stay in business. Cash generated through the sale of fixed assets is not sustainable. Eventually, the assets will be gone.

Cash Flow Statement

	2011
Investing Activities	
Capital expenditures	-3,541
Business acquisitions	-2,000
Purchase/sale of equity investments	1,400
Purchase/sale of short-term investments	-1,100
Net cash used in investing activities	$ -5,241

Figure 52

Another important activity is to determine how much of the operating cash flow is being spent on replacement capital expenditures. If the company has to spend the majority of what it makes from operations on replacing fixed assets in order to stay in business, this is not a good sign because it will not have any cash left for growth. In this case, investors should not expect to do well owning the stock of such a company.

FINANCING ACTIVITIES

Cash flows from financing activities involve transactions that affect the company's owners or creditors, such as issuing stock, repurchasing shares, paying dividends, and issuing or repaying debt. These transactions are not reflected in net income, but because they affect cash, they need to appear on the cash flow statement as shown in Figure 53.

Cash Flow Statement

	2011
Operating Activities	
Net income	$ 8,732
Adjustments to reconcile net income to net cash provided by operating activities:	
Depreciation expense	2,123
Gain/loss on sale of fixed assets	89
Changes in operating assets and liabilities:	
Accounts receivable	2,312
Inventories	-1,100
Prepaid expenses and other current assets	110
Accounts payable	1,068
Accrued expenses	-987
Income taxes payable	-60
Net cash provided by operating activities	$ 12,287
Investing Activities	
Capital expenditures	-3,541
Business acquisitions	-2,000
Purchase/sale of equity investments	1,400
Purchase/sale of short-term investments	-1,100
Net cash used in investing activities	$ -5,241
Financing Activities	
Borrowing/repayment of long-term debt	-3,389
Issuance of common stock	0
Stock repurchases	-2,000
Cash dividends paid	-3,000
Net cash (used in) provided by financing activities	$ -8,389
Net (decrease) increase in cash and cash equivalents	-1,343
Cash and cash equivalents at beginning of year	4,273
Cash and cash equivalents at end of year	$ 2,930

Figure 53

BORROWING/REPAYMENT OF LONG-TERM DEBT

The borrowing and repayment of long-term debt is pretty straightforward. A positive number on the cash flow statement means that the company received money, while a negative number means that it paid the balance down. Companies in high-growth stages are more likely to have positive cash flow from long-term debt because they tend to borrow to finance their current operations and future growth. Companies that generate significant operating cash flow are in a position where they can finance their operations and growth internally. In addition, they are likely to show negative cash flow from long-term debt because they are using the internally generated cash to repay it.

Cash Flow Statement

	2011
Financing Activities	
Borrowing/repayment of long-term debt	-3,389
Issuance of common stock	0
Stock repurchases	-2,000
Cash dividends paid	-3,000
Net cash (used in) provided by financing activities	$ -8,389

Figure 54

The borrowing or repayment of long-term debt in a particular reporting period only shows an incremental increase or decrease in the outstanding debt balance.

For the total amount of debt, investors need to review the balance sheet.

ISSUANCE OF COMMON STOCK

When companies go public and issue or sell shares to shareholders, they report this action as a positive cash flow in the financing activities section of the cash flow statement because cash is being received from buyers of these shares. The same effect occurs when the company issues additional shares. High-growth companies are more likely to engage in issuing additional shares because their operations have not yet generated sufficient cash. While the shareholders' equity on the balance sheet is increased when new shares are issued, shareholders' existing interests are being diluted unless they take part in the new issuance.

Cash Flow Statement

	2011
Financing Activities	
Borrowing/repayment of long-term debt	-3,389
Issuance of common stock	0
Stock repurchases	-2,000
Cash dividends paid	-3,000
Net cash (used in) provided by financing activities	$ -8,389

Figure 55

SHARE REPURCHASES

Share repurchases are the opposite of share issuances. A company that engages in share repurchases is spending cash, and therefore, the cash effect on the cash flow statement is negative. While share repurchases increase the ownership interests of existing shareholders, they are only beneficial when the company's stock is purchased at a good price. It does not benefit the existing shareholders if the management repurchases the company's stock for $20 per share when it is only worth $5 per share. The situation becomes even worse when the management borrows money to repurchase overpriced stock. The best scenario occurs when the company generates a positive operating cash flow and the management uses a portion of it to repurchase shares that are undervalued, or at least, valued fairly. To determine how much a company's management paid per share to repurchase shares, investors can reference the company's annual report (10-k).

Cash Flow Statement

	2011
Financing Activities	
Borrowing/repayment of long-term debt	-3,389
Issuance of common stock	0
Stock repurchases	-2,000
Cash dividends paid	-3,000
Net cash (used in) provided by financing activities	$ -8,389

Figure 56

CASH DIVIDENDS PAID

Cash dividends paid are pretty straightforward. They create a negative or neutral cash effect because the company either pays them or does not pay them. High-growth companies usually do not pay any dividends because they are reinvesting every penny they make back into their businesses, and the rate of return on those investments is believed by management to be favorable.

Cash Flow Statement

	2011
Financing Activities	
Borrowing/repayment of long-term debt	-3,389
Issuance of common stock	0
Stock repurchases	-2,000
Cash dividends paid	-3,000
Net cash (used in) provided by financing activities	$ -8,389

Figure 57

Dividends can provide shareholders with current income, and dividend-paying companies usually attract retirees who rely on dividend income to pay bills. The key with dividend income is to determine its safety and dependability. If a company is earning enough money to cover the dividend, it is unlikely that the dividend will be eliminated. However, if the company is not earning it and relies on the sale of assets or external borrowing to keep paying it, this is a red flag because these sources of cash are not as dependable as operational cash flow. A good rule of thumb for investors who want to determine the safety of a dividend (risk of a dividend cut) is to compare net cash provided by operating activities ($12,287 in Figure 53) with cash dividends paid ($3,000 in Figure 57). Cash provided by operations being two to three times the size of dividends usually indicates that the risk of a dividend cut is low, as is the case in our example. A dividend cut can cause the stock price to collapse because investors who depend on the dividend income to pay bills are likely to sell it when the dividend is taken away. Safe and dependable dividends can create support for the stock price because if the price decreases, the dividend yield increases (dividend yield = dividend per share/ price per share), thus attracting investors back into the stock. For opportunistic investors, a dividend cut can create a great buying opportunity when the dividend elimination is only temporary. When the dividend is reinstated, the stock price will likely recover.

NET CASH (USED IN) PROVIDED BY FINANCING ACTIVITIES

Net cash (used in) provided by financing activities is the sum of all the financing cash flows. It is more likely to be positive for high-growth companies than for mature ones. As mentioned before, high-growth companies are not usually in a position to pay dividends or repurchase shares because they keep reinvesting everything they make back into their businesses. They might even borrow more money and issue additional shares to accelerate their growth. Mature companies that pay dividends and repurchase shares tend to show a negative cash flow from financing activities.

Cash Flow Statement

	2011
Financing Activities	
Borrowing/repayment of long-term debt	-3,389
Issuance of common stock	0
Stock repurchases	-2,000
Cash dividends paid	-3,000
Net cash (used in) provided by financing activities	$ -8,389

Figure 58

If a business is generating a negative operating cash flow and a positive financing cash flow, they are engaging in an activity that is not sustainable in the long term. At some point, lenders or new investors are going to stop providing the company with new capital.

SUMMARY

The cash flow statement records various cash movements during the reporting period. By classifying them into cash provided or used by operating activities, investing activities, and financing activities, investors are in a better position to determine whether the cash is generated from renewable sources, such as operations, or non-recurring sources, such as fixed asset sales, and whether cash is being spent on acquiring additional fixed assets, making share repurchases, or paying dividends.

The three financial statements – the balance sheet, the income statement, and the cash flow statement – all serve different purposes. One might be more suited to determine the company's profitability, and another might be better for showing the company's assets. They should all be studied together because they are connected, and by analyzing these relationships, investors are able to uncover the economics of particular businesses and decide if purchasing or selling them are prudent choices.

Conclusion

Chapter 4

Conclusion

The basic knowledge of accounting, which is the language of business, will allow you to read and finally understand what the management of a company is communicating to you through their financial statements. At the beginning of this book, the following text was presented:

"Jeśli rozwiniesz swoje umiejętności inwestycyjne i jeśli inwestujesz mądrze, to pozwoli Ci to w przyszłości żyć lepiej i zapewnisz sobie w ten sposób godną emeryturę na przyszłość. Niestety większość ludzi nie ma ochoty uczyć się jak inwestować swoje pieniądze, więc dlatego ufają na ślepo tak zwanym profesjonalistom, którzy są ubrani w drogie i eleganckie garnitury, są dobrze uczesani i pięknie mówią. Drogę, którą wybierzesz, zależy wyłącznie od Ciebie."

By learning basic accounting principles, you acquire the ability to translate financial statements into comprehensible information, just as learning Polish would allow you to translate the text above into the following:

"If you take the time to develop your investing skills, and if you invest your money wisely, it can work hard for you and allow you to enjoy a better life and a carefree retirement. However, many do not educate themselves, and instead, blindly follow the advice of a sleek-looking and fast-talking Wall Street salesperson dressed in an expensive suit. Which path you follow depends on you."

I hope you found this book to be educational and helpful, and I also hope that it will only be the beginning and not the end of your investment education. For my recommendations of other books to read, please refer to next page. For a more complete list, visit my blog at www.classicvalueinvestors.com.

Sincerely,

Mariusz Skonieczny

RECOMMENDED BOOKS

Why Are We So Clueless about the Stock Market: Learn how to invest your money, how to pick stocks, and how to make money in the stock market by Mariusz Skonieczny

Financial Statements: A Step-by-Step Guide to Understanding and Creating Financial Reports by Thomas R. Ittelson

The Interpretation of Financial Statements by Benjamin Graham and Spencer B. Meredith

Financial Shenanigans: How to Detect Accounting Gimmicks & Fraud in Financial Reports by Howard M. Schilit and Jeremy Perler

Creative Cash Flow Reporting: Uncovering Sustainable Financial Performance by Charles W. Mulford and Eugene E. Comiskey

Quality of Earnings by Thornton L. O'glove

The Financial Numbers Game: Detecting Creative Accounting Practices by Charles W. Mulford and Eugene E. Comiskey

Warren Buffett and the Interpretation of Financial Statements: The Search for the Company with a Durable Competitive Advantage by Mary Buffett and David Clark

Hidden Financial Risk: Understanding Off Balance Sheet Accounting by J. Edward Ketz

Financial Fine Print: Uncovering a Company's True Value by Michelle Leder